John W. Schaum

Level Five

Chord Speller

for Piano, Electronic Keyboard or Organ

Foreword

The Schaum Chord Speller is a comprehensive workbook that teaches every fundamental chord plus all of the important altered chords. The four basic triads: major, minor, augmented and diminished are thoroughly explained. Major and minor "added-sixth" chords are carefully analyzed. A wide variety of seventh chords is presented including the dominant, diminished, major, minor, augmented and the minor-seventh with diminished fifth. Ninth chords receive special attention. Chord construction in all its many phases and a new enlarged chord dictionary are additional features. This outstanding book is a *must* for every student interested in harmony.

Contents

Lesson	page
1. Major Triads	2
2. Minor Triads	3
3. Augmented Triads	4
4. Major Triad Inversions	5
5. Minor Triad Inversions	6
6. Augmented Triad Inversions	7
7. Major Scale Triads	8
8. Triad Identification	9
9. Major Sixth Chords	10
10. Minor Sixth Chords	11
11. Dominant Seventh Chords	12
12. Dominant Seventh Inversions	13
13. Diminished Seventh Chords	14
14. Enharmonic Diminished Sevenths	15
15. Major Seventh Chords	16
16. Minor Seventh Chords	17
17. Minor Seventh (Diminished 5th)	18
18. Augmented Seventh Chords	19
19. Major Scale Seventh Chords (Part 1)	20
20. Major Scale Seventh Chords (Part 2)	21
21. Dominant Ninth Chords	22
22. Chord Construction	23
Chord Dictionary	24

Progressive Succession of Schaum Workbooks:
Theory Workbook, Level 2
Rhythm Workbook, Level 2
Easy Keyboard Harmony, Book 1 (Level 2)
Scale Speller (Level 2)
Theory Workbook, Level 3
Rhythm Workbook, Level 3
Easy Keyboard Harmony, Book 2 (Level 3)
Arpeggio Speller (Level 3)
Easy Keyboard Harmony, Book 3 (Level 4)
Interval Speller (Level 4)
Easy Keyboard Harmony, Book 4 (Level 5)
Chord Speller (Level 5)
Easy Keyboard Harmony, Book 5 (Level 6)

Schaum Publications, Inc. •  EXCLUSIVELY DISTRIBUTED BY

7777 W. BLUEMOUND RD. P.O. BOX 13819 MILWAUKEE, WI 53213

© Copyright 1967 by Schaum Publications, Inc., Mequon, Wisconsin
International Copyright Secured • All Rights Reserved • Printed in U.S.A.
ISBN-13: 978-1-936098-16-3

Warning: The reproduction of any part of this publication without prior written consent of Schaum Publications, Inc. is prohibited by U.S. Copyright Law and subject to penalty. This prohibition includes all forms of printed media (including any method of photocopy), all forms of electronic media (including computer images), all forms of film media (including filmstrips, transparencies, slides and movies), all forms of sound recordings (including cassette tapes and compact disks), and all forms of video media (including video tapes and DVD).

Lesson 1. Major Triads

Pupil's Name.. Completion Date..
Assignment Date.................................... Grade or Star..

A CHORD is a combination of three or more tones. The term TRIAD designates a three-tone CHORD. The major triad is made up of the first (root), third and fifth tones of the major scale. Analytically, it consists of a major third and a perfect fifth. (1,3,5)

DIRECTIONS: Below are the twelve major scales. First, take a pencil and fill in the 1st, 3rd and 5th notes of each scale; then write the three notes of each major triad in the blank measures. Use whole notes. Study the example.

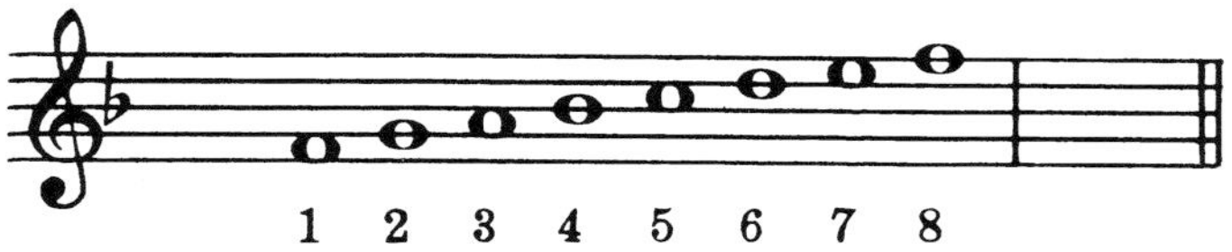

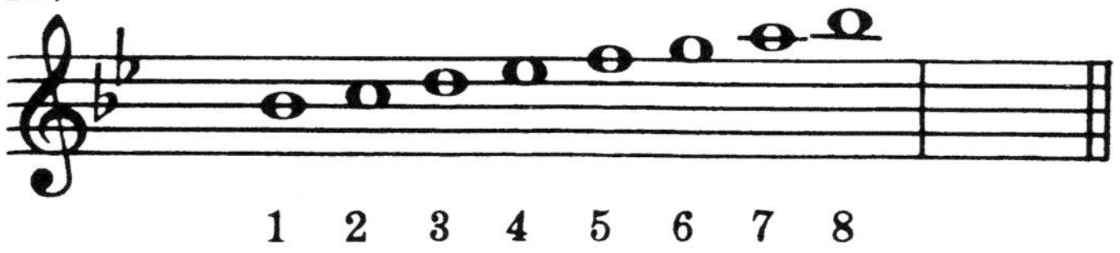

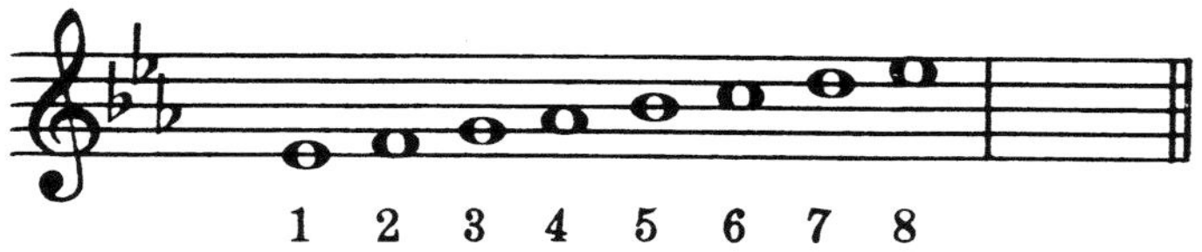

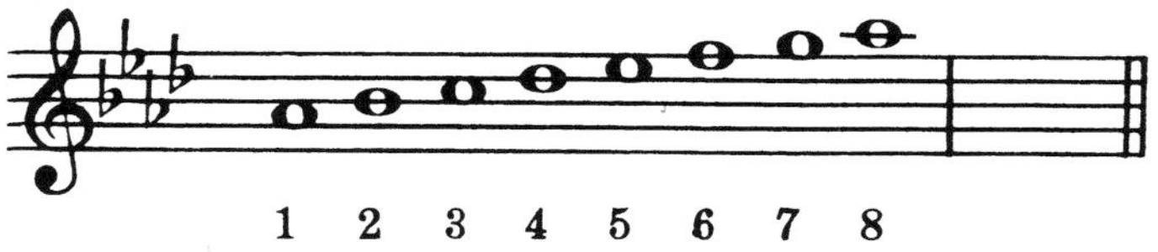

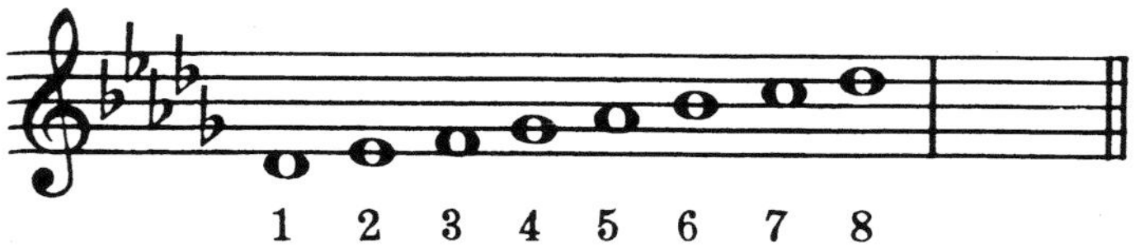

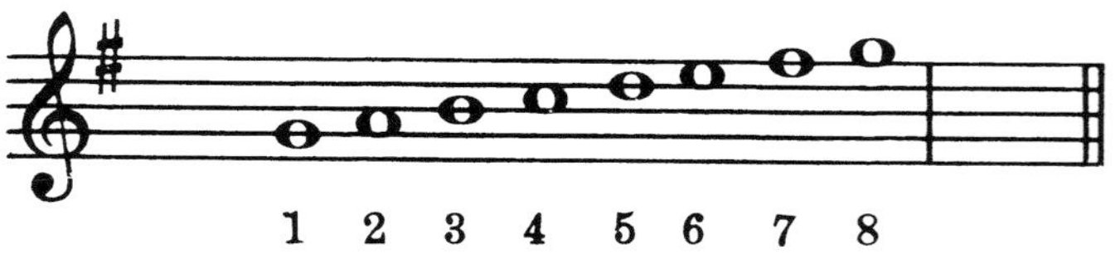

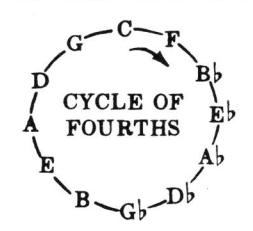

CYCLE OF FOURTHS

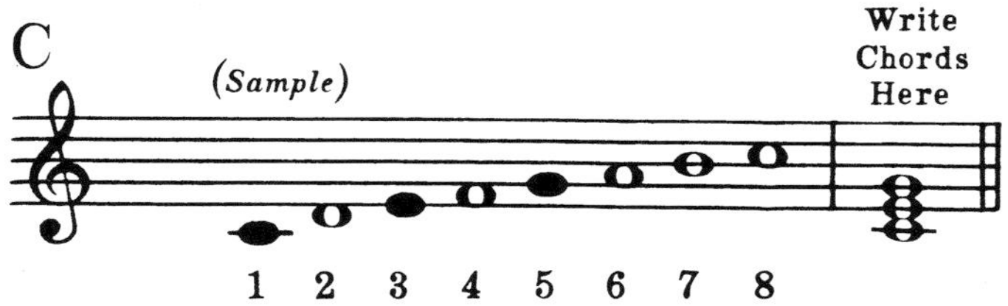

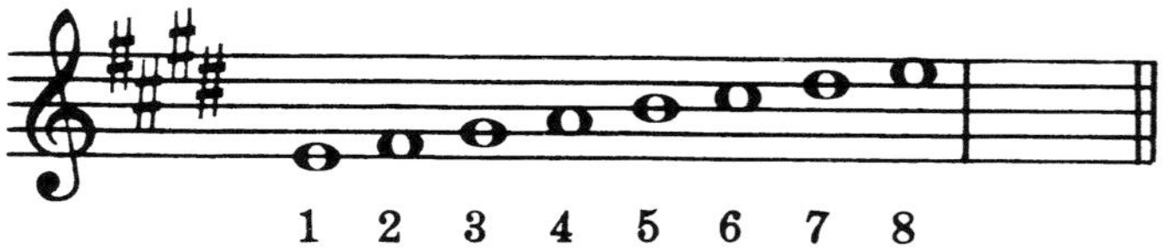

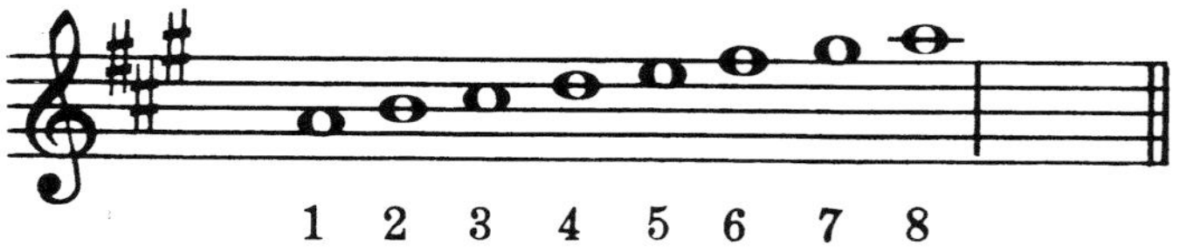

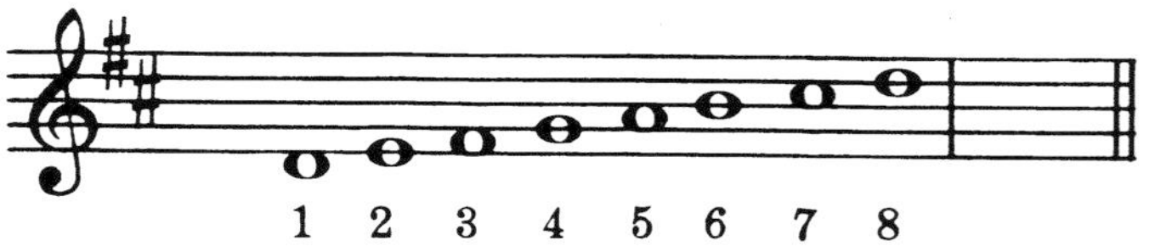

In vocal and in instrumental music, chords frequently follow one another in order of FOURTHS. Consequently, in the John W. Schaum CHORD SPELLER, the chords are presented according to the cycle of fourths.

Teacher's Note: As a pre-requisite to the John W. Schaum CHORD SPELLER, the student should have completed both the Schaum "Scale Speller" and the Schaum "Interval Speller."

Lesson 2. Minor Triads

Pupil's Name.. Completion Date..
Assignment Date.. Grade or Star..

A minor triad (symbol=m) is formed by lowering the middle tone of a major chord one half-step. Analytically it consists of a minor third and a perfect fifth. (1, 3♭, 5)

DIRECTIONS: On the staffs below, insert the necessary accidental signs (♯, ♭, etc.) so that the notes in every measure correctly represent each minor triad. Write letter names on dotted lines.

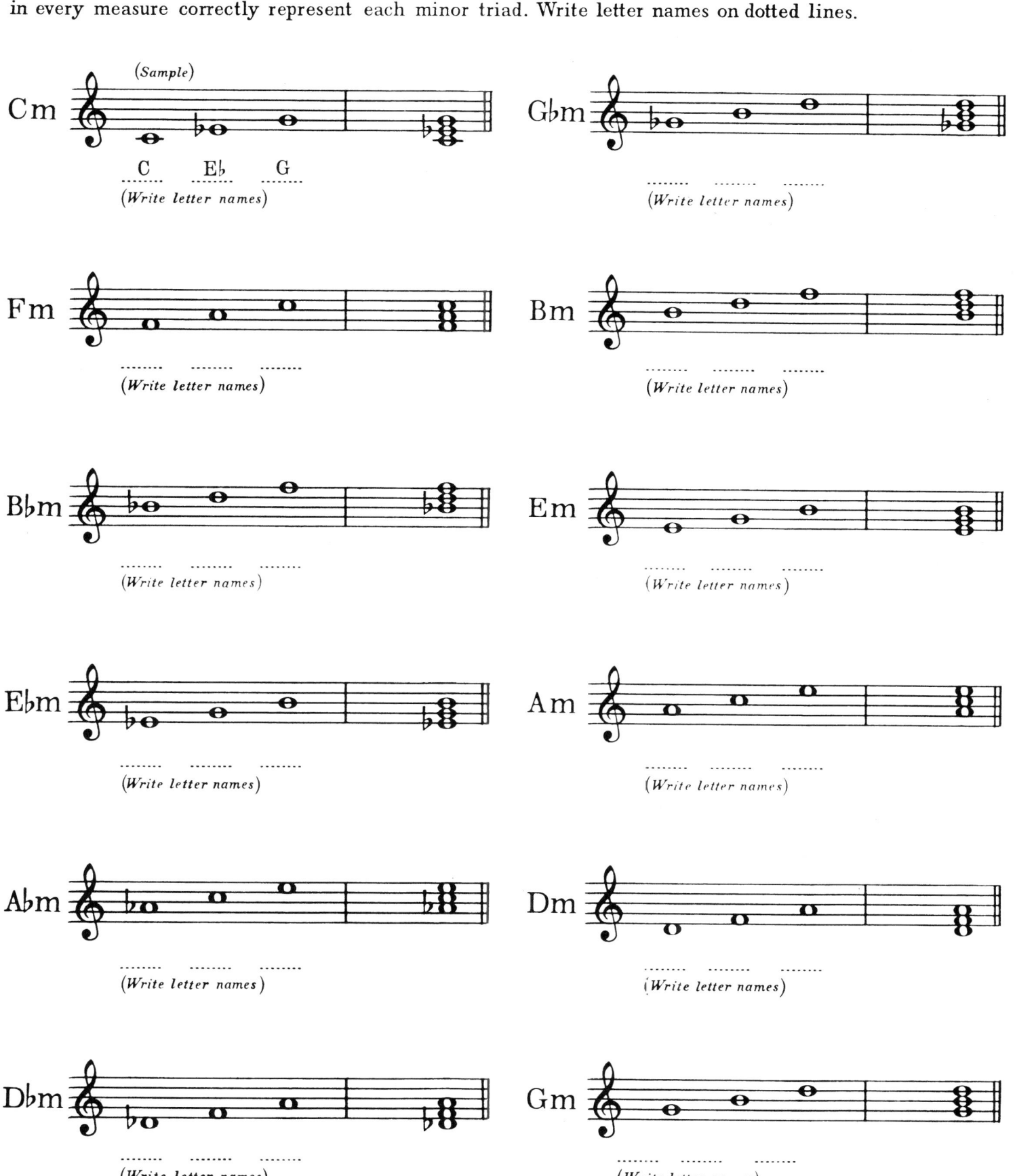

Lesson 3. Augmented Triads

Pupil's Name...................................... Completion Date......................................
Assignment Date.................................. Grade or Star...

An augmented triad (symbol = +) is formed by raising the upper tone of the major triad one half-step. Analytically it consists of a major third and an augmented fifth. (1, 3, 5♯)

DIRECTIONS: In the following measures, insert the necessary accidental signs (♯, ♭, etc.) so that the notes in every measure correctly represent each augmented triad. Write letter names on the dotted lines.

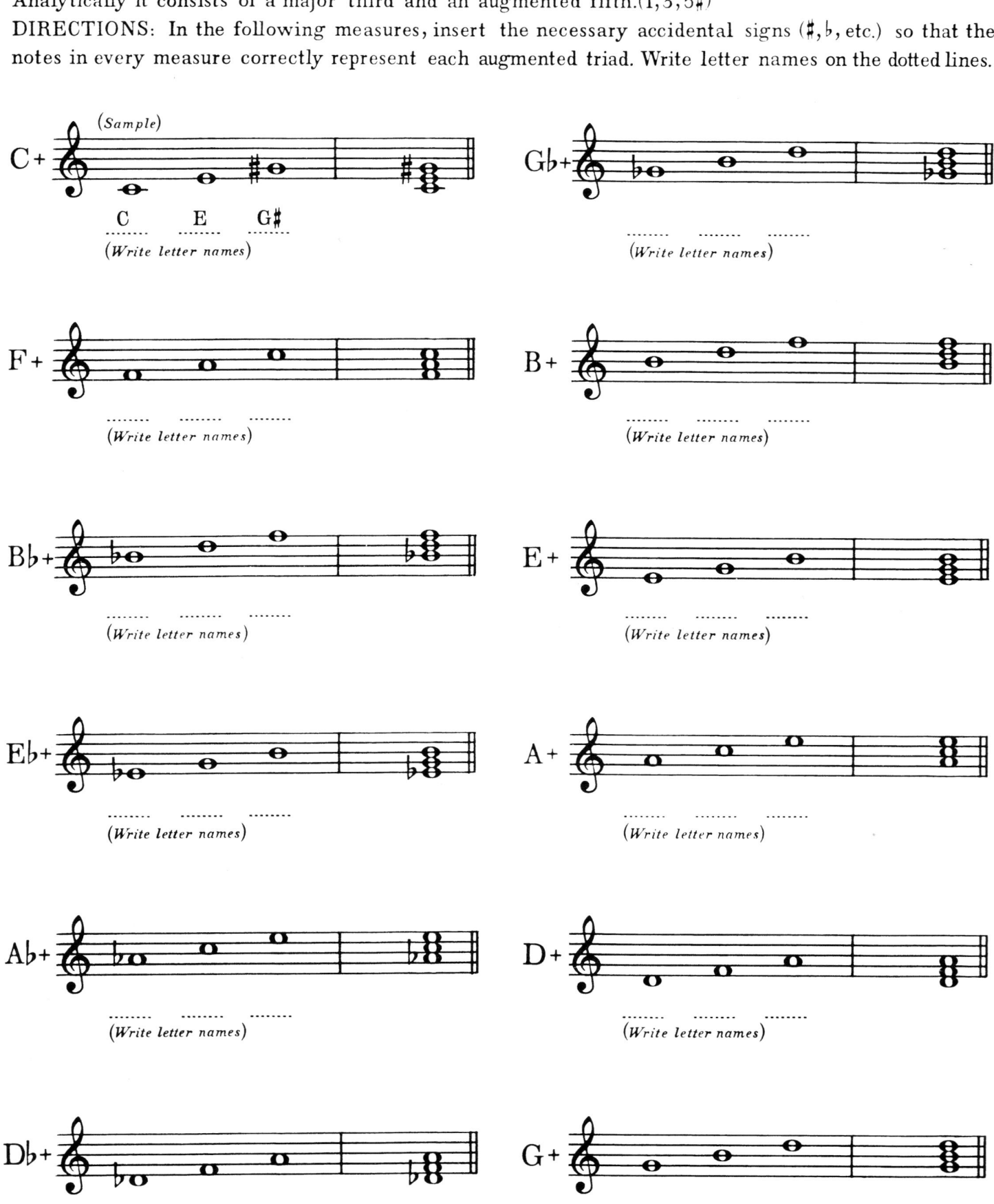

Lesson 4. Major Triad Inversions

Pupil's Name.................. Completion Date..................
Assignment Date.................. Grade or Star..................

When the three tones of a triad are regrouped into different positions—they are called inversions. Every triad has two inversions. See sample.

DIRECTIONS: On the staffs below, write the first and second inversion for each major triad. Use whole notes. Write letter names in the blank boxes below each chord.

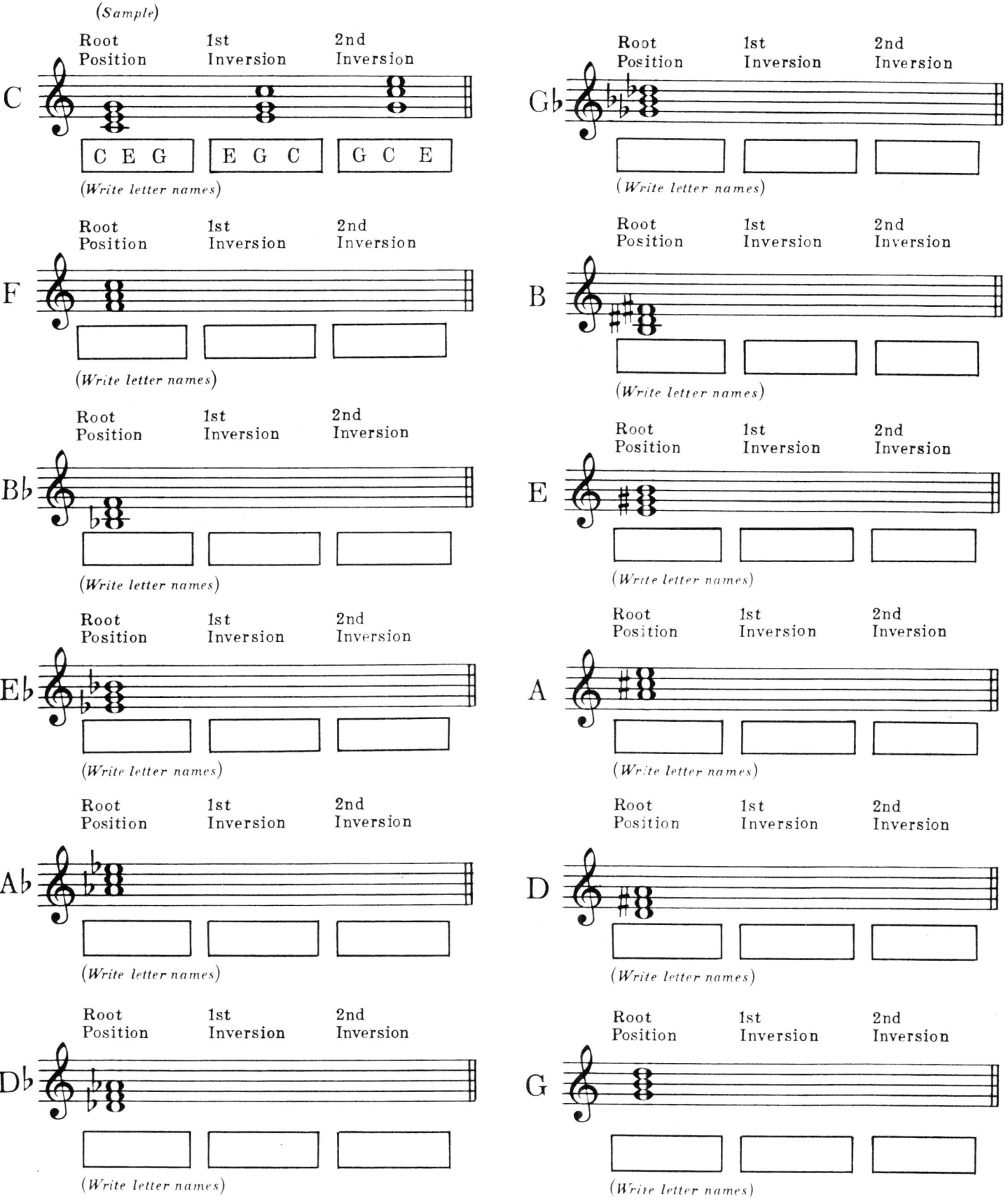

Lesson 5. Minor Triad Inversions

Pupil's Name.. Completion Date..
Assignment Date...................................... Grade or Star...

DIRECTIONS: On the staffs below, write the first and second inversion for each minor triad. Use whole notes. Write letter names in the blank boxes below each chord.

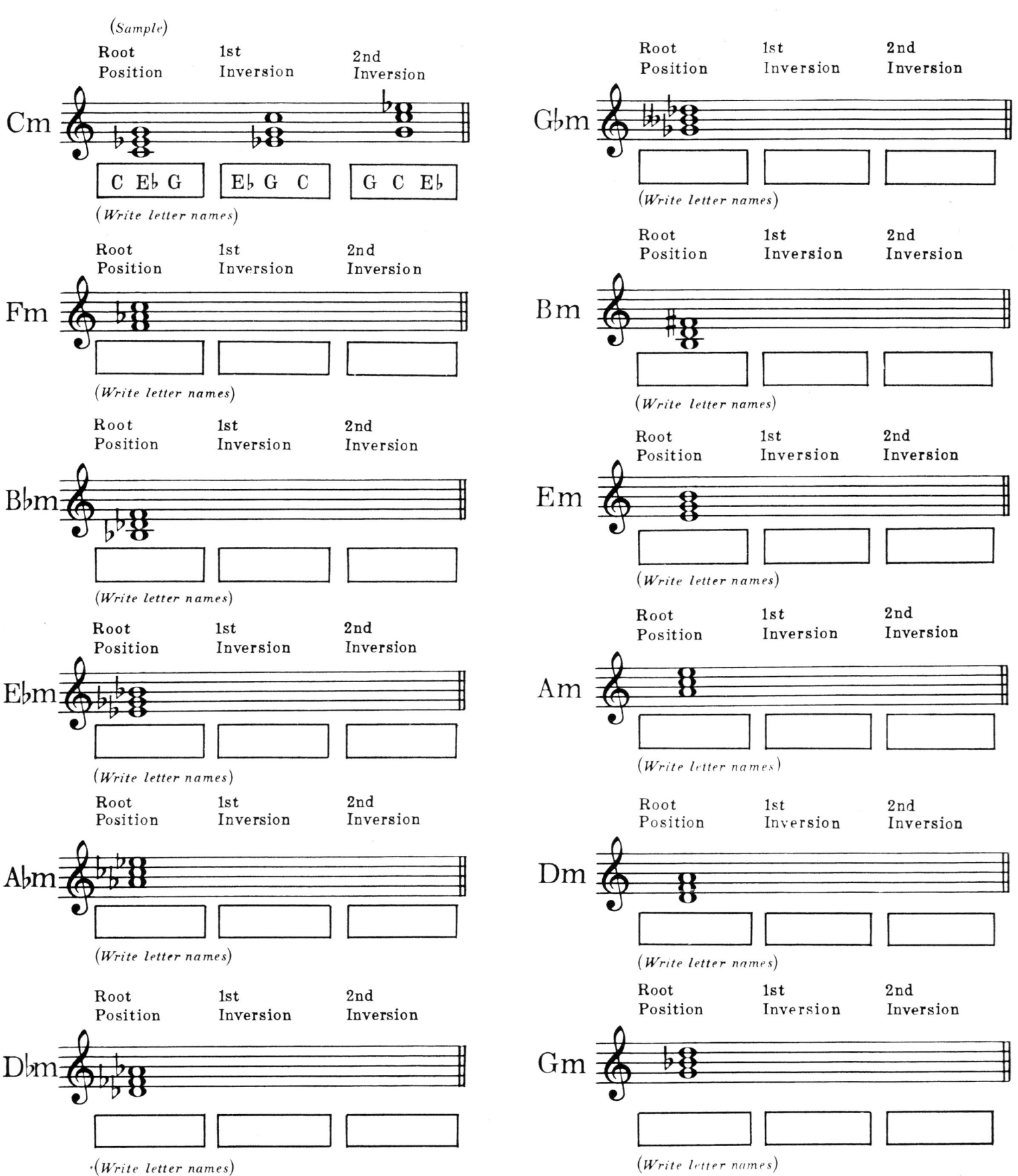

Lesson 6. Augmented Triad Inversions

Pupil's Name.. Completion Date..
Assignment Date.. Grade or Star..

DIRECTIONS: On the staffs below, write the first and second inversion for each augmented triad. Use whole notes. Write letter names in the blank boxes below each chord.

(Sample)

C+ — Root Position: C E G♯ | 1st Inversion: E G♯ C | 2nd Inversion: G♯ C E

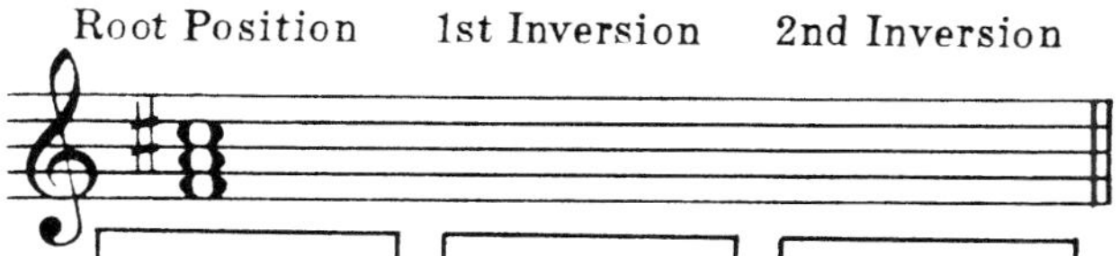

F+ — Root Position | 1st Inversion | 2nd Inversion

B♭+ — Root Position | 1st Inversion | 2nd Inversion

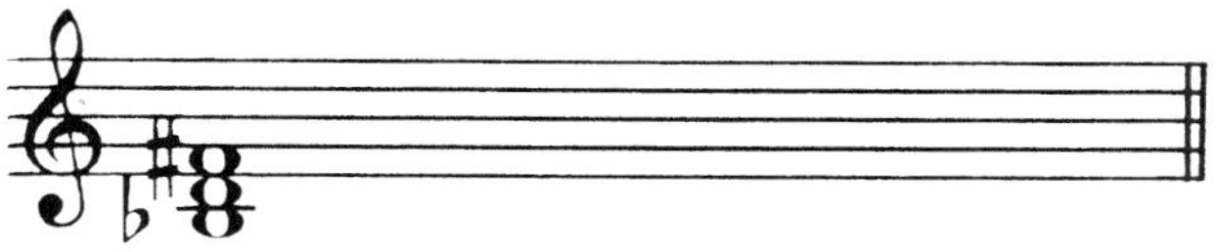

E♭+ — Root Position | 1st Inversion | 2nd Inversion

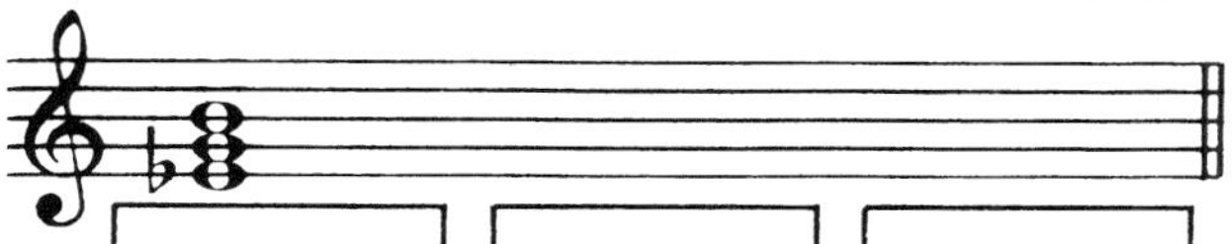

A♭+ — Root Position | 1st Inversion | 2nd Inversion

D♭+ — Root Position | 1st Inversion | 2nd Inversion

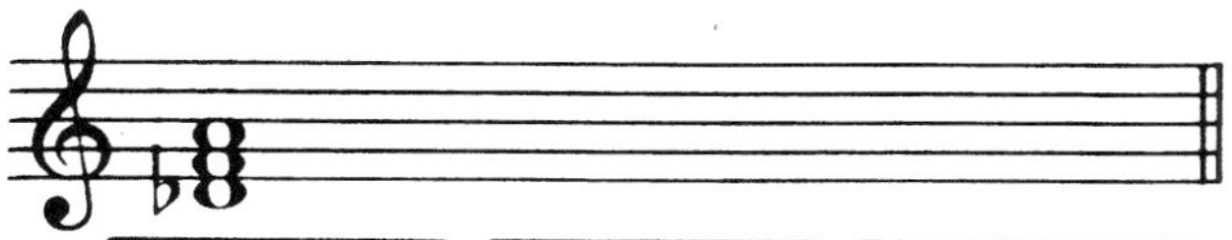

G♭+ — Root Position | 1st Inversion | 2nd Inversion

B+ — Root Position | 1st Inversion | 2nd Inversion

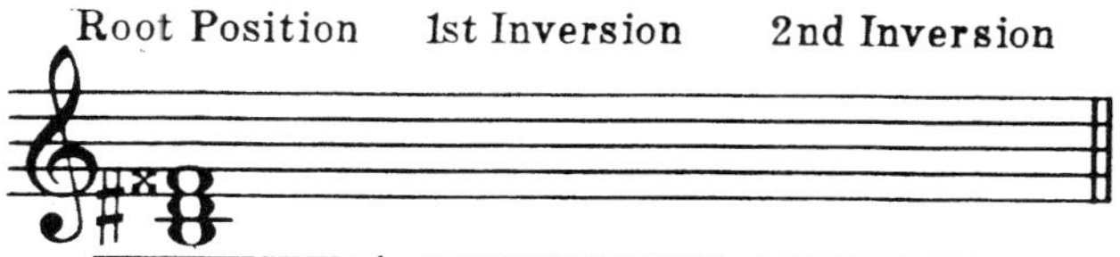

E+ — Root Position | 1st Inversion | 2nd Inversion

A+ — Root Position | 1st Inversion | 2nd Inversion

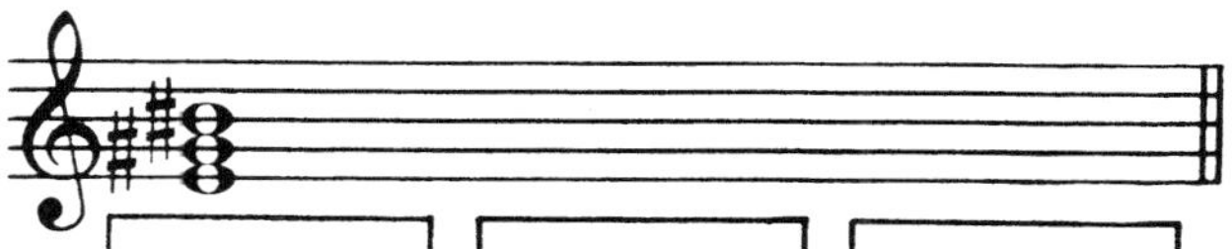

D+ — Root Position | 1st Inversion | 2nd Inversion

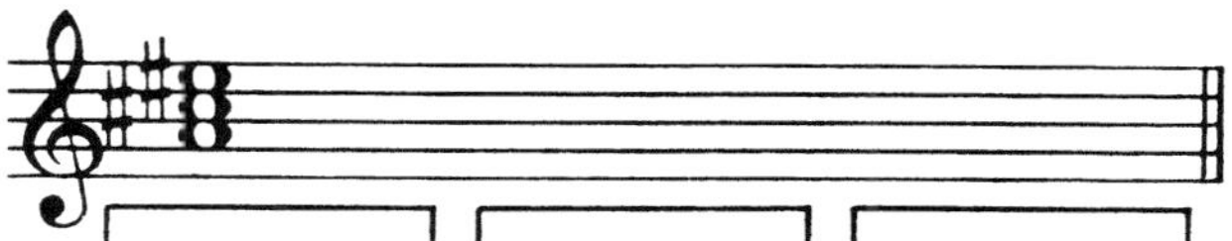

G+ — Root Position | 1st Inversion | 2nd Inversion

Note: Actually, there are only four augmented triads. Study the chart below, and notice how the twelve chords of the cycle are reduced to inversions of the four basic triads at the top of each column.

1. { C E G♯ / A♭ C E / E G♯ B♯ }
2. { F A C♯ / D♭ F A / A C♯ E♯ }
3. { B♭ D F♯ / G♭ B♭ D / D F♯ A♯ }
4. { E♭ G B / B D♯ F𝄪 / G B D♯ }

Lesson 7. Major Scale Triads

Pupil's Name.. Completion Date..
Assignment Date.. Grade or Star..

DIRECTIONS: On the following staffs, write a triad above each scale degree. Use whole notes. Then write the letter symbol name of each triad on the dotted lines. Study the example.

Note: A new triad occurs on the seventh degree of the scale. It is called a *diminished* triad (symbol = small zero sign after the letter name). Analytically it consists of a minor third and a diminished fifth. (1, 3♭, 5♭)

The inversions of the diminished triad are not being presented since they are rarely used. Instead, the diminished seventh chords are used. See pages 14 and 15.

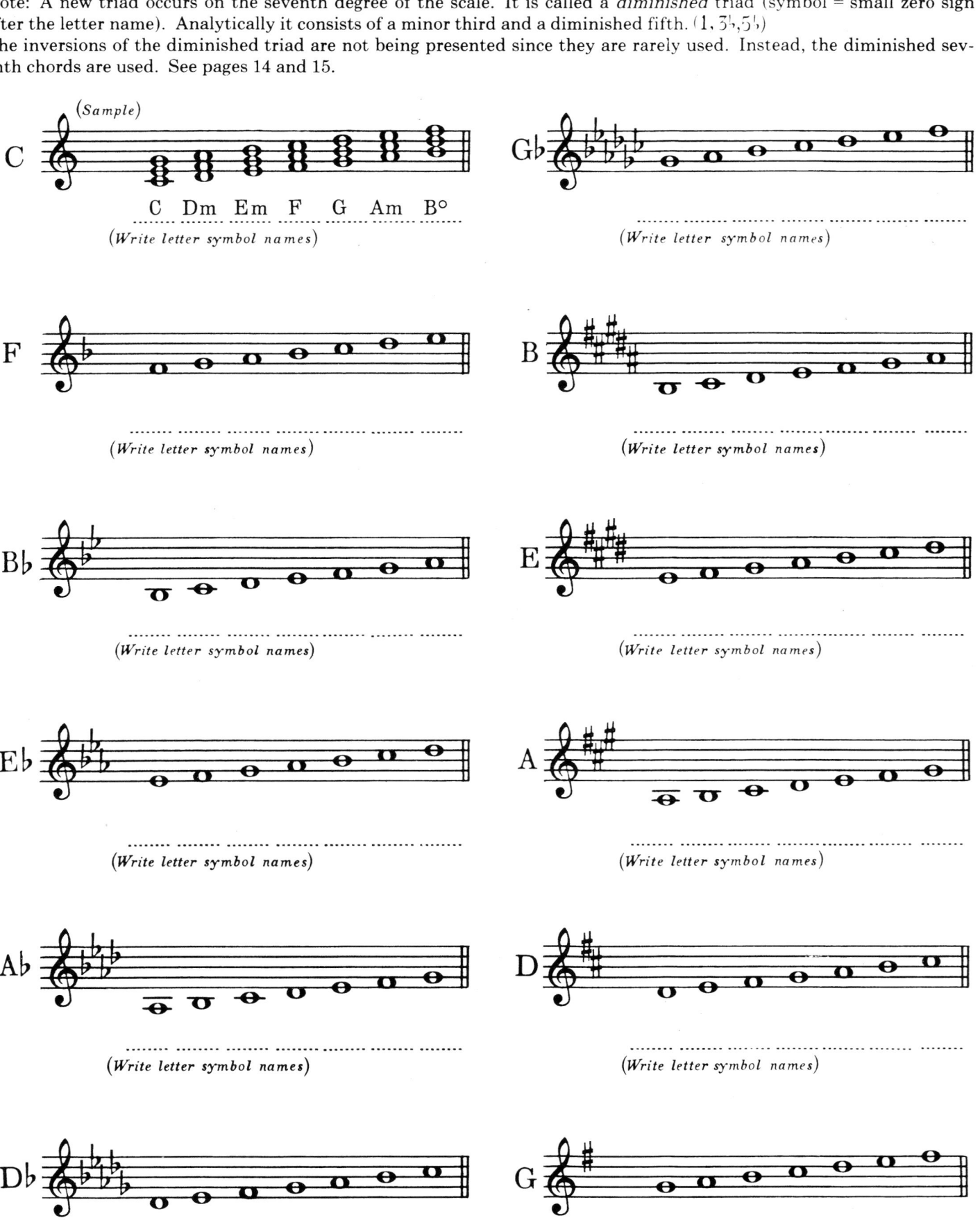

Lesson 8. Triad Identification

Pupil's Name.. Completion Date..
Assignment Date.. Grade or Star...

DIRECTIONS: Below is a series of various triads. Write the correct letter symbol names on the dotted lines. Study the samples.

(Samples)

F   E♭°   Cm   A+   ....

Lesson 9. Major Sixth Chords

Pupil's Name.. Completion Date..
Assignment Date.. Grade or Star...

A major sixth chord (symbol=6) is formed by adding a major sixth to the major triad. Analytically, it consists of a major third, a perfect fifth and a major sixth. (1,3,5,6)

DIRECTIONS: On the following staffs, insert the necessary accidental signs (♯, ♭, etc.) so that the notes in every measure correctly represent each major sixth chord. Write letter names on dotted lines.

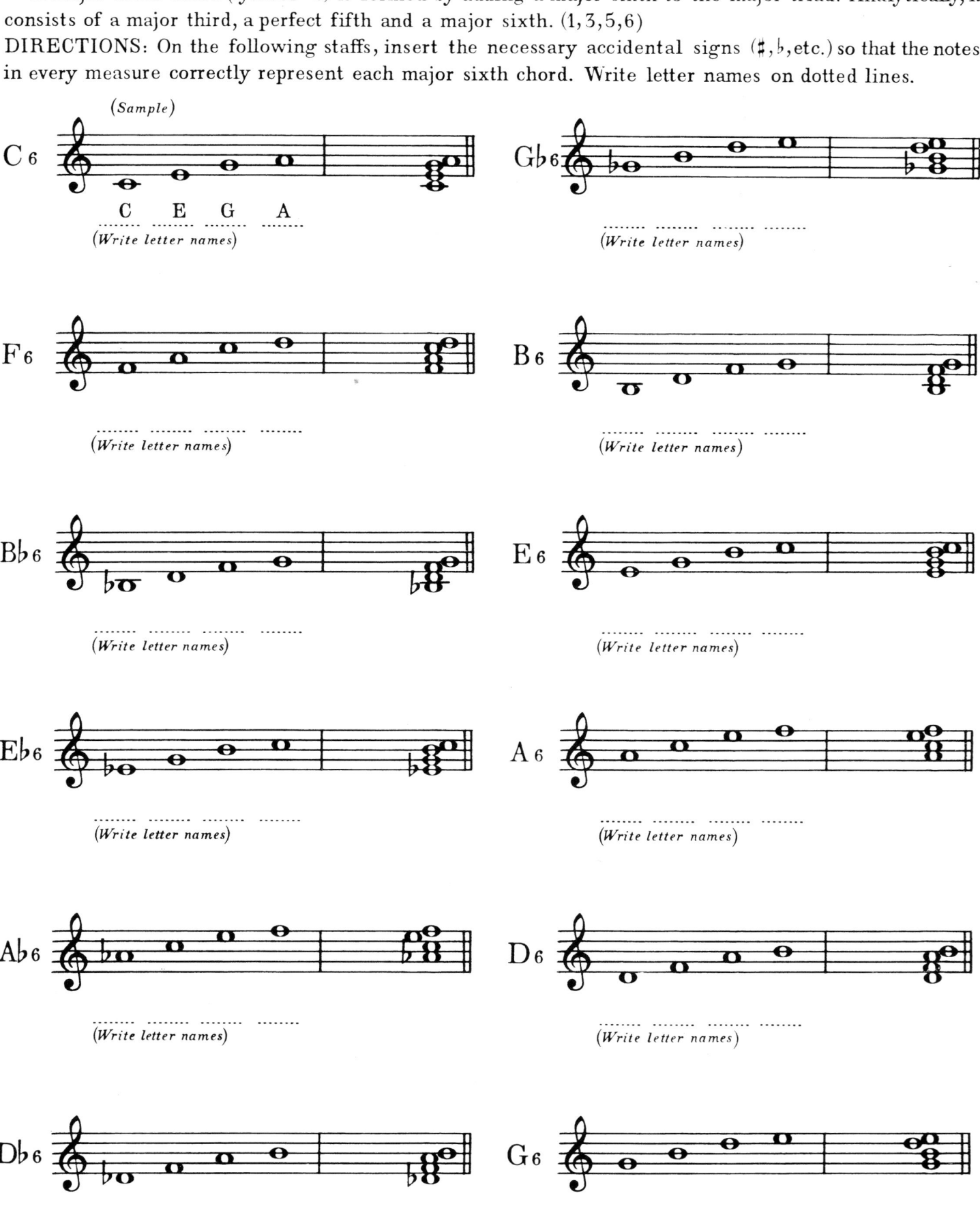

Lesson 10. Minor Sixth Chords

Pupil's Name..   Completion Date..
Assignment Date...   Grade or Star..

A minor sixth chord (symbol = m6) is formed by adding a major six to the MINOR triad. Analytically, it consist of a minor third, a perfect fifth and a major sixth (1, 3♭, 5, 6)

DIRECTIONS: On the staffs below, insert the necessary accidental signs (♯, ♭, etc.) so that the notes in every measure correctly represent each minor sixth chord. Write letter names on dotted lines.

Cm6 — (Sample)   C   E♭   G   A   *(Write letter names)*

Gbm6 — *(Write letter names)*

Fm6 — *(Write letter names)*

Bm6 — *(Write letter names)*

B♭m6 — *(Write letter names)*

Em6 — *(Write letter names)*

E♭m6 — *(Write letter names)*

Am6 — *(Write letter names)*

A♭m6 — *(Write letter names)*

Dm6 — *(Write letter names)*

D♭m6 — *(Write letter names)*

Gm6 — *(Write letter names)*

Lesson 11. Dominant Seventh Chords

Pupil's Name.. Completion Date..
Assignment Date.. Grade or Star...

A dominant seventh chord (symbol=7) consists of four tones. It is formed by adding a minor seventh to a major triad. Analytically, it is composed of a major third, a perfect fifth and a minor seventh. (1,3, 5,7♭)

DIRECTIONS: On the staffs below, insert the necessary accidental signs (♯,♭,etc.) so that the notes in each measure correctly represent the dominant seventh chord. Write letter names on dotted lines.

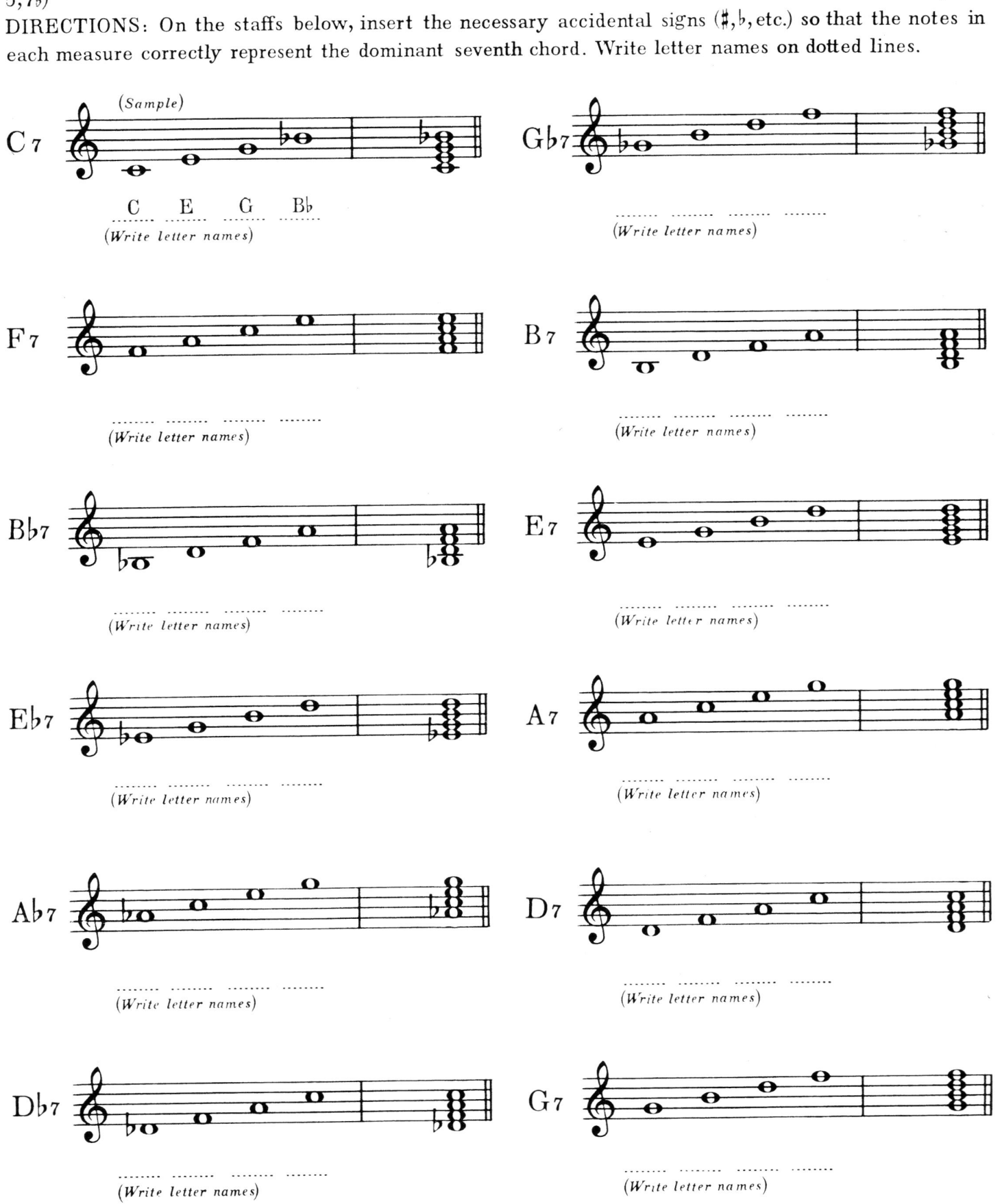

Lesson 12. Dominant Seventh Inversions

Pupil's Name.. Completion Date..
Assignment Date... Grade or Star..

DIRECTIONS: On the staffs below, write the three inversions for each dominant seventh chord. Use whole notes. Write letter names in the blank boxes below each chord.

(Sample)

C7 — Root Position | 1st Inversion | 2nd Inversion | 3rd Inversion

| C E G B♭ | E G B♭ C | G B♭ C E | B♭ C E G |

(Write letter names)

F7 — Root Position, 1st Inversion, 2nd Inversion, 3rd Inversion
(Write letter names)

B♭7 — Root Position, 1st Inversion, 2nd Inversion, 3rd Inversion
(Write letter names)

E♭7 — Root Position, 1st Inversion, 2nd Inversion, 3rd Inversion
(Write letter names)

A♭7 — Root Position, 1st Inversion, 2nd Inversion, 3rd Inversion
(Write letter names)

D♭7 — Root Position, 1st Inversion, 2nd Inversion, 3rd Inversion
(Write letter names)

G♭7 — Root Position, 1st Inversion, 2nd Inversion, 3rd Inversion
(Write letter names)

B7 — Root Position, 1st Inversion, 2nd Inversion, 3rd Inversion
(Write letter names)

E7 — Root Position, 1st Inversion, 2nd Inversion, 3rd Inversion
(Write letter names)

A7 — Root Position, 1st Inversion, 2nd Inversion, 3rd Inversion
(Write letter names)

D7 — Root Position, 1st Inversion, 2nd Inversion, 3rd Inversion
(Write letter names)

G7 — Root Position, 1st Inversion, 2nd Inversion, 3rd Inversion
(Write letter names)

Lesson 13. Diminished Seventh Chords

Pupil's Name.. Completion Date..
Assignment Date.. Grade or Star..

A diminished seventh chord (symbol = *dim.*) contains four tones. It is built up in minor thirds. Each of the four tones is a minor third apart. (1, 3♭, 5♭, 7♭♭)

DIRECTIONS: On the following staffs, insert the necessary accidental signs (♯, ♭, etc) so that the notes in each measure correctly represent the diminished seventh chord. Write letter names on dotted lines.

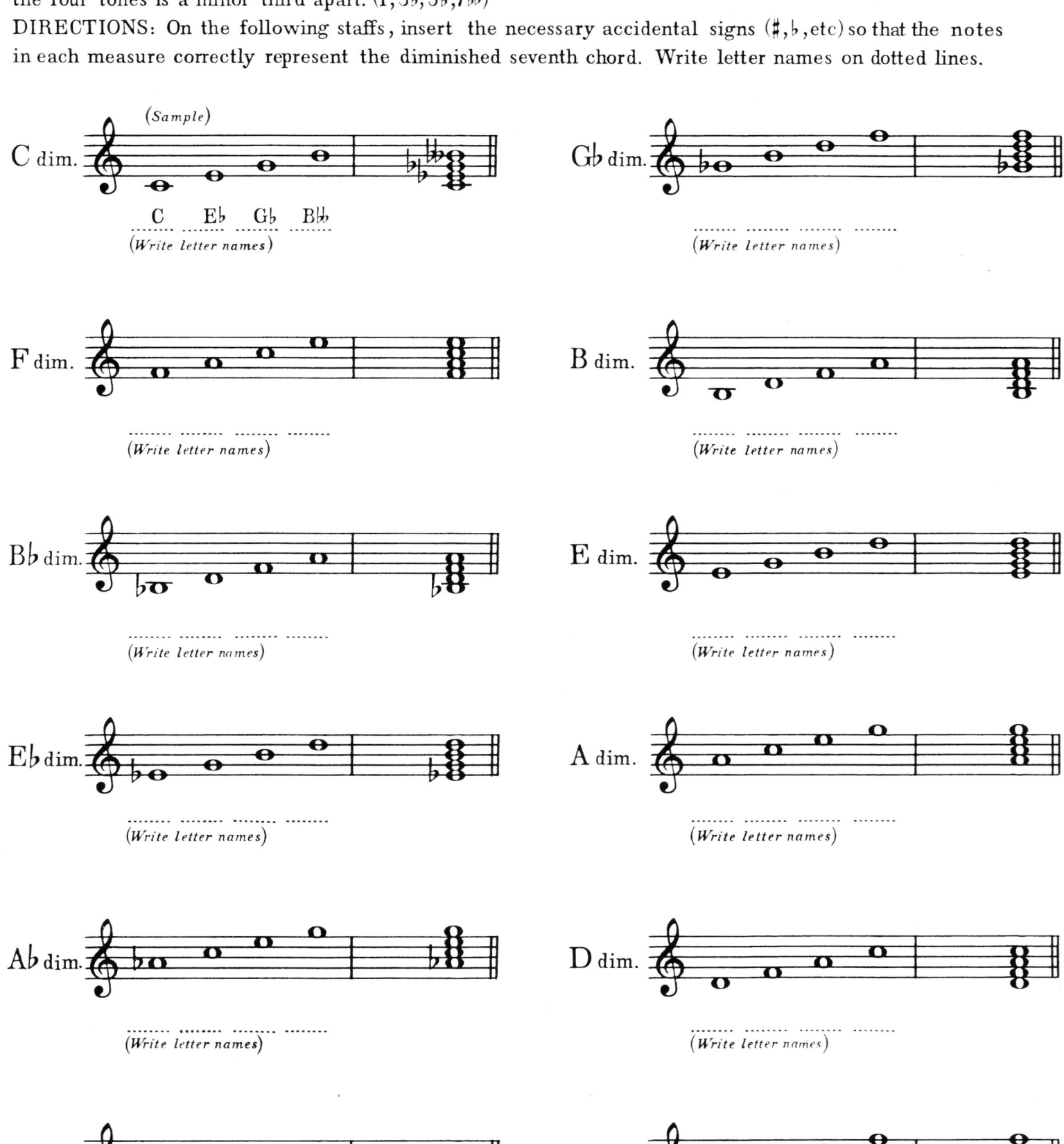

Lesson 14. Enharmonic Diminished Sevenths

Pupil's Name.. Completion Date..
Assignment Date.. Grade or Star...

Diminished seventh chords are frequently spelled differently than in Lesson Thirteen. This is done to simplify the reading by eliminating many of the accidental signs. When the same series of tones is written in another form, it is called an enharmonic change. In like manner, there are words in our language which sound alike but have different spellings. For example: earn and urn, pain and pane, herd and heard, etc.

DIRECTIONS: Enharmonic spellings of the various diminished seventh chords appear on the staffs below. Insert the correct letter names on the dotted lines.

FIRST SET

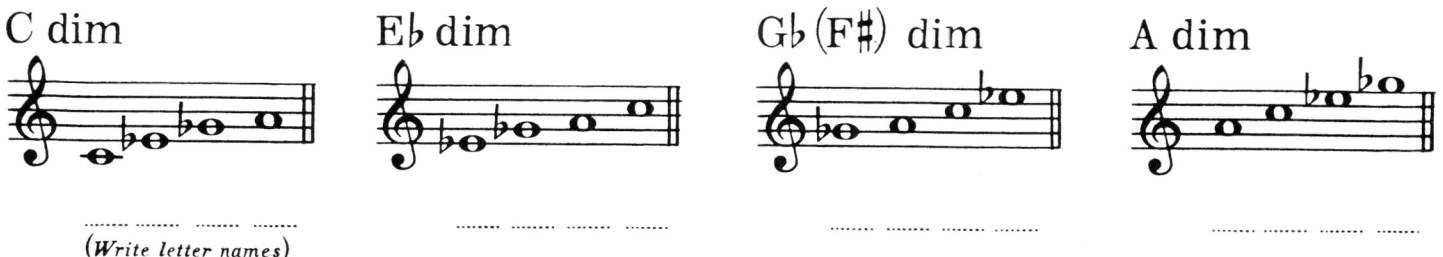

(Write letter names)

SECOND SET

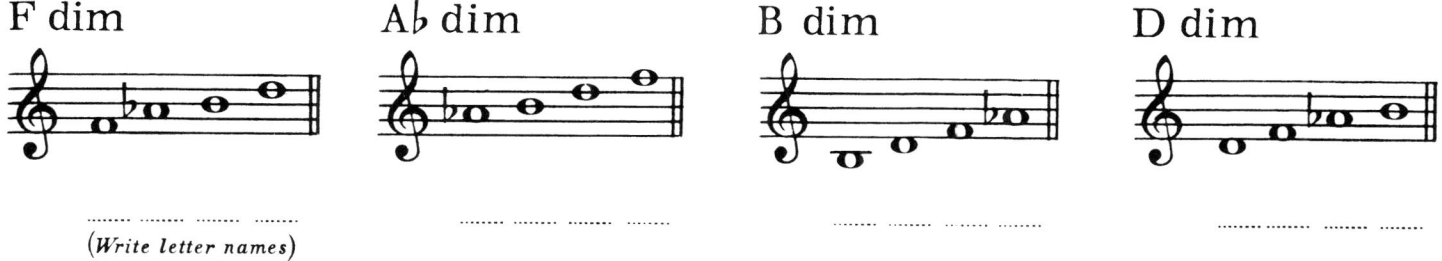

(Write letter names)

THIRD SET

(Write letter names)

Note: There are actually only three diminished seventh chords. Observe in the FIRST SET above, how all four chords are in reality inversions of one another. This is also true of sets two and three.

Lesson 15. Major Seventh Chords

Pupil's Name.. Completion Date..
Assignment Date.. Grade or Star...

A major seventh chord (symbol = maj 7) is composed of four tones. It is made by adding a major seventh to a major triad. Analytically, it consists of a major third, a perfect fifth and a major seventh. (1, 3, 5, 7)

DIRECTIONS: On the following staffs, put in the essential accidental signs (♯, ♭, etc.) so that the notes in each measure accurately represent the major seventh chord. Write letter names on dotted lines.

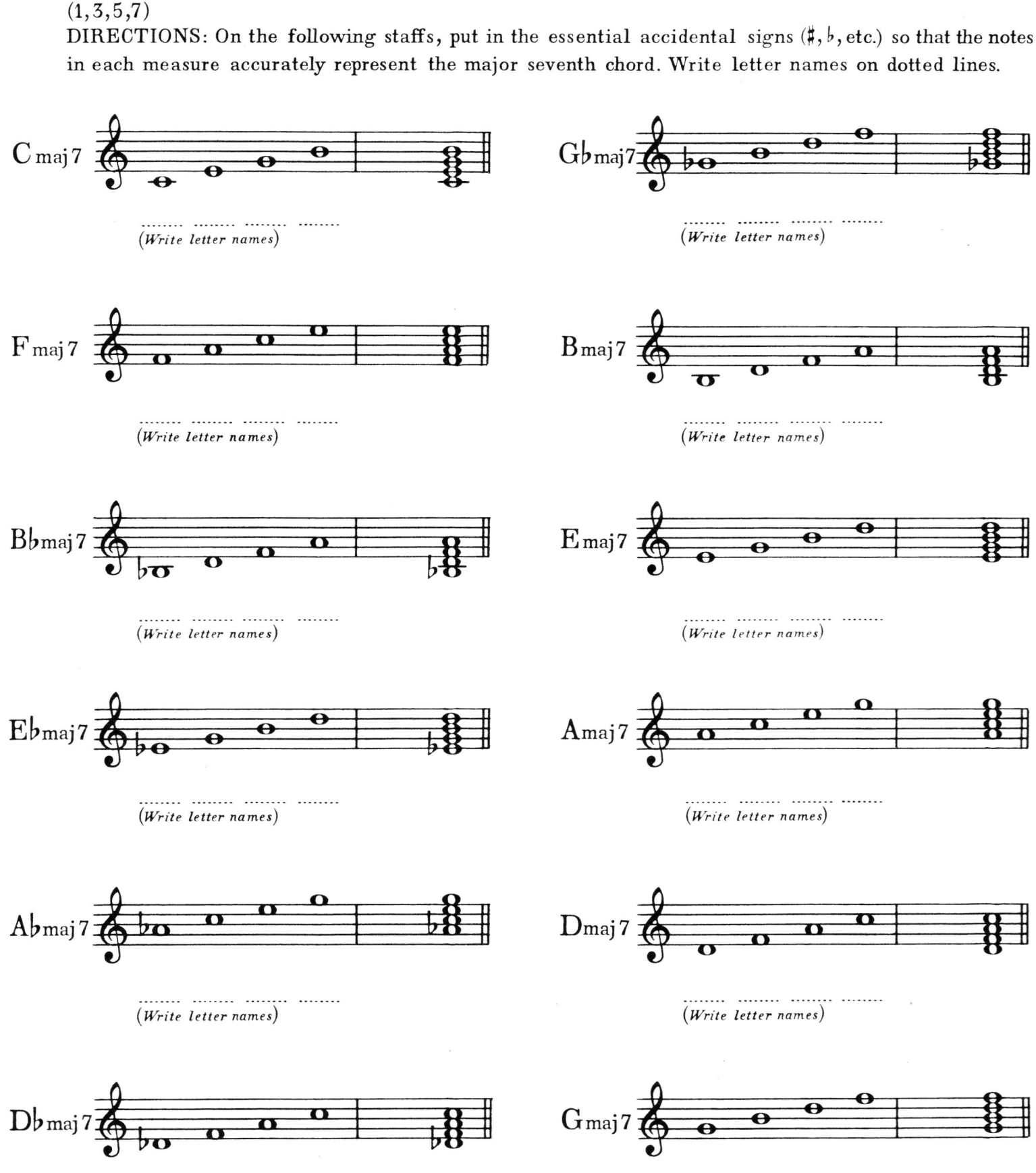

Lesson 16. Minor Seventh Chords

Pupil's Name.. Completion Date..
Assignment Date.. Grade or Star..

A minor seventh chord (symbol=m7) is a four tone chord that is made by adding a **minor** seventh to a minor triad. Analytically, it consists of a minor third, a perfect fifth and a minor seventh. (1, 3♭, 5, 7♭)

DIRECTIONS: On the following staffs, put in the required accidental signs (♯, ♭, etc.) so that the notes in each measure **precisely** represent the minor seventh chord. Write letter names on dotted lines.

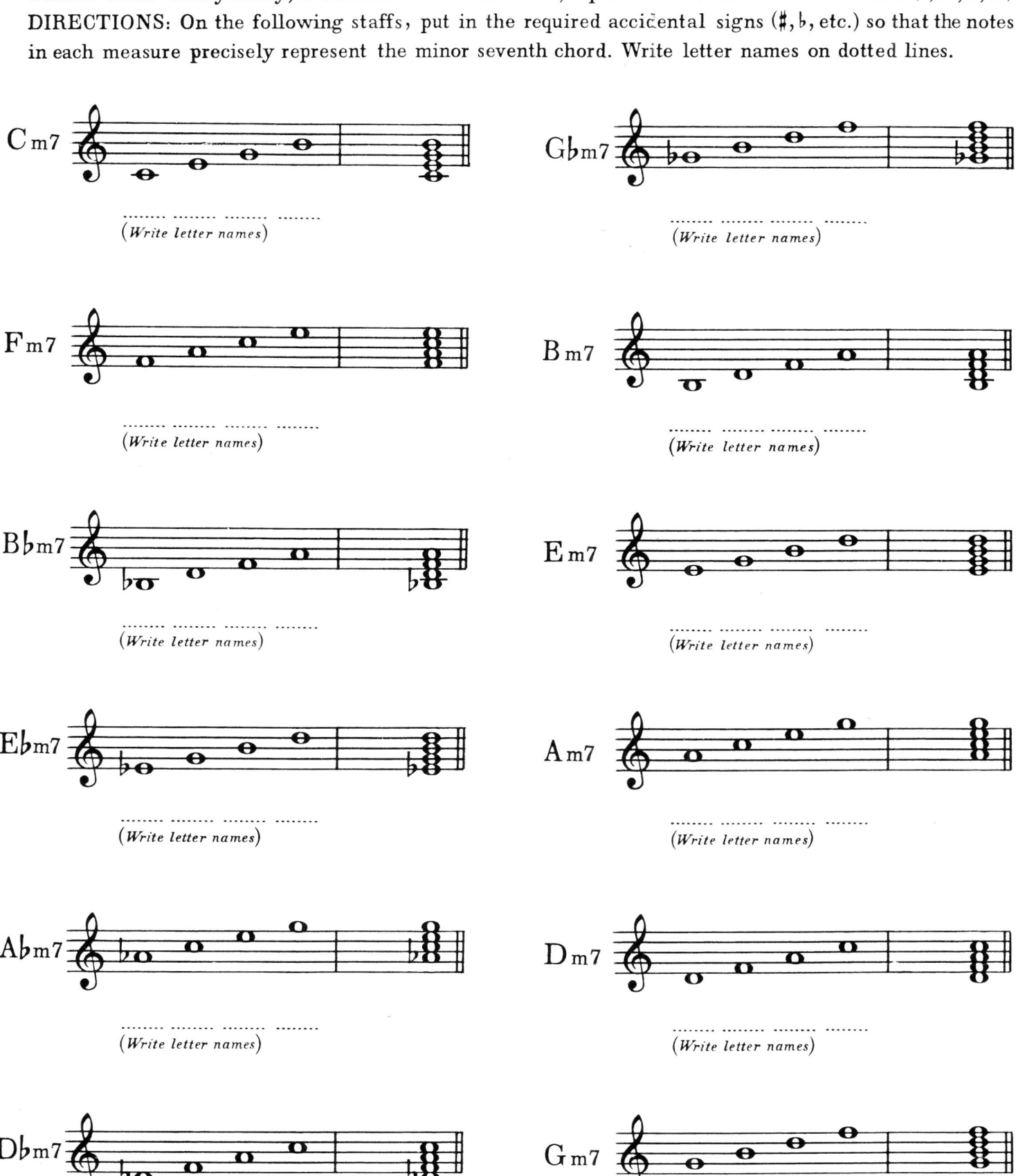

Lesson 17. Minor Seventh (Diminished 5th)

Pupil's Name.. Completion Date..
Assignment Date.. Grade or Star..

A minor seventh chord with a diminished fifth (symbol=m7-5)* consists of a minor third, a diminished fifth and a minor seventh. (1, 3♭, 5♭, 7♭)

DIRECTIONS: On the following staffs, place the proper accidental signs (♯, ♭, etc.) so that the notes in each measure accurately represent the minor seventh chord with a diminished fifth. Write letter names on dotted lines.

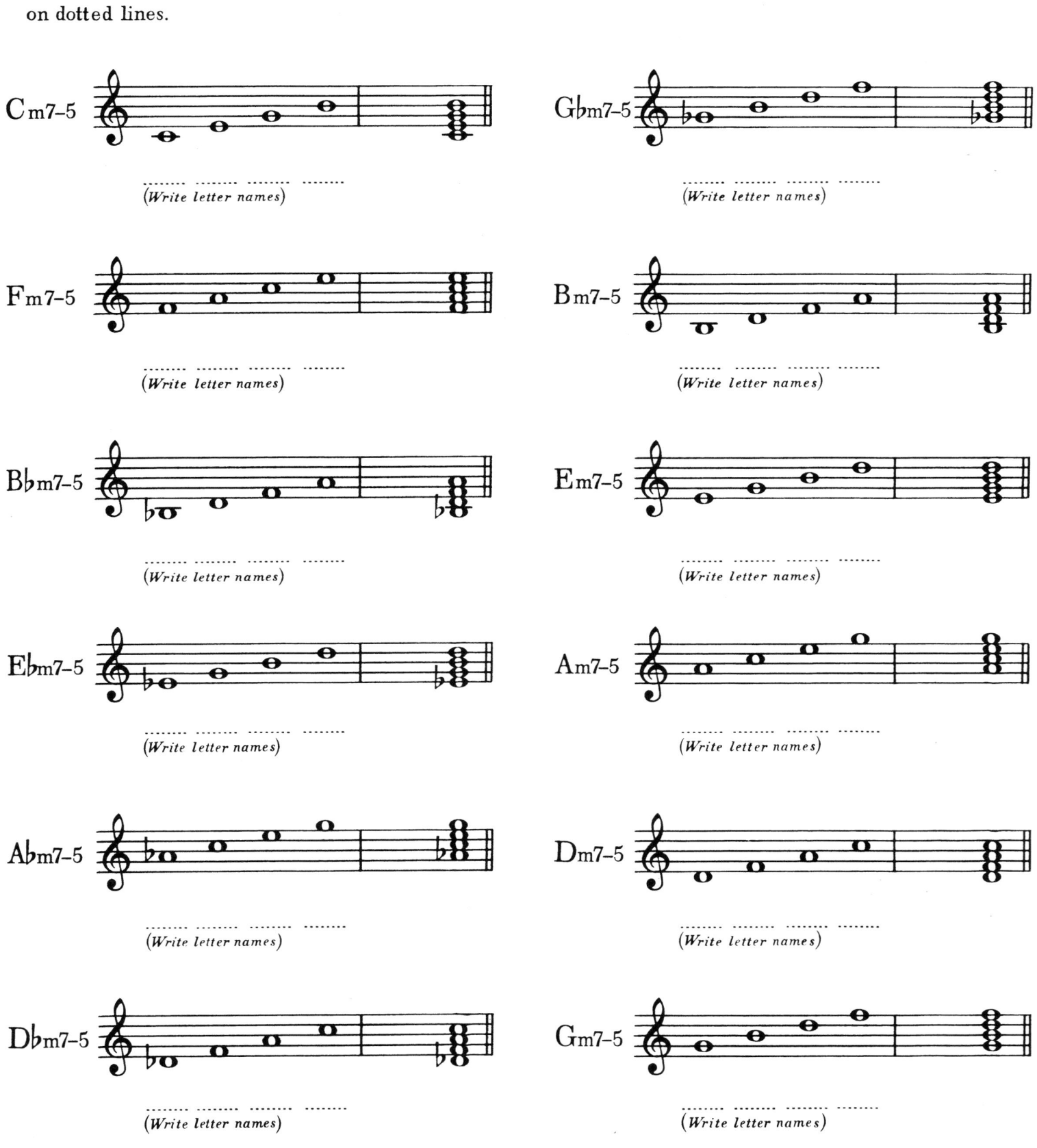

*Note: The minus five (-5) symbol is sometimes depicted as 5♭ and means to lower the fifth a half step.

Lesson 18. Augmented Seventh Chords

Pupil's Name.. Completion Date..................................
Assignment Date... Grade or Star.....................................

An augmented seventh chord (symbol = +7) is made up of a major third, an augmented fifth and a minor seventh. (1, 3, 5♯, 7♭)

DIRECTIONS: On the staffs below, insert the correct accidental signs (♯, ♭, etc.) so that the notes in each measure precisely depict the augmented seventh chord. Write letter names on dotted lines.

C+7
(Write letter names)

G♭+7
(Write letter names)

F+7
(Write letter names)

B+7
(Write letter names)

B♭+7
(Write letter names)

E+7
(Write letter names)

E♭+7
(Write letter names)

A+7
(Write letter names)

A♭+7
(Write letter names)

D+7
(Write letter names)

D♭+7
(Write letter names)

G+7
(Write letter names)

Lesson 19. Major Scale Seventh Chords (Part 1)

Pupil's Name.. Completion Date..
Assignment Date.. Grade or Star..

DIRECTIONS: On the following staffs, write a seventh chord above each scale degree. Use whole notes. Then write the letter symbol name of each seventh chord on the dotted lines. Study the sample.

C (Sample)

Cmaj7 Dm7 Em7 Fmaj7 G7 Am7 Bm7−5
(Write letter symbol names)

F

(Write letter symbol names)

B♭

(Write letter symbol names)

E♭

(Write letter symbol names)

A♭

(Write letter symbol names)

D♭

(Write letter symbol names)

Lesson 20. Major Scale Seventh Chords (Part 2)

Pupil's Name.. Completion Date..
Assignment Date.. Grade or Star..

DIRECTIONS: On the following staffs, write a seventh chord above each scale degree. Use whole notes. Then write the letter symbol name of each seventh chord on the dotted lines. Study the sample.

Gb

(Write letter symbol names)

B

(Write letter symbol names)

E

(Write letter symbol names)

A

(Write letter symbol names)

D

(Write letter symbol names)

G

(Write letter symbol names)

Lesson 21. Dominant Ninth Chords

Pupil's Name.. Completion Date..
Assignment Date....................................... Grade or Star...

A dominant ninth chord (symbol = 9) is a five tone chord that is formed by adding a major ninth to a dominant seventh chord. Analytically it consists of a major third, a perfect fifth, a minor seventh and a major ninth. (1, 3, 5, 7♭, 9)

DIRECTIONS: On the following staffs, place the necessary accidental signs (♯, ♭, etc.) that will correctly convert the notes in each measure to a dominant ninth chord.

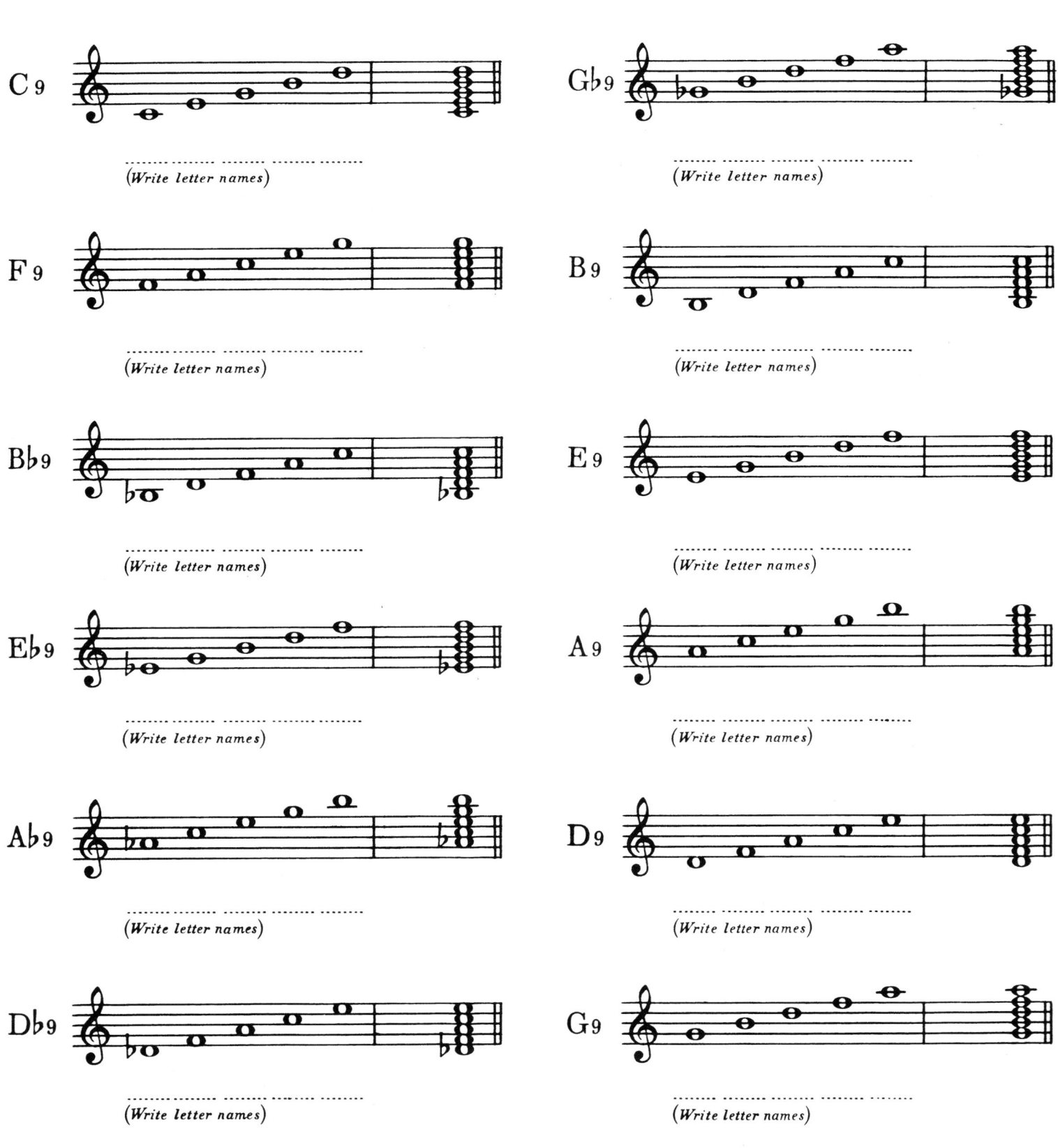

Lesson 22. Chord Construction

Pupil's Name... Completion Date..
Assignment Date.. Grade or Star..

Each type of chord is built according to a very exact formula. The major scale is the foundation on which chords are constructed. For example, to form a major chord, use the 1st, 3rd and 5th tones of the major scale. All chords originate from the basic major scale tones. Many of these tones are often modified or altered to produce a variety of colorful harmonies. The pattern for each chord is shown in the chart below.

To aid in the formation of chords in all keys, the twelve major scales are also included in the chart. For F♯ chords use G♭; for C♯ chords use D♭; for G♯ chords use A♭; for D♯ chords use E♭.

TYPE OF CHORD	ABBREVIATION	Scale Degree Chord Patterns	MAJOR SCALES 1 2 3 4 5 6 7 8
C Major	C	1, 3, 5	C .... C D E F G A B C
C Minor	Cm	1, 3♭, 5	D♭ .... D♭ E♭ F G♭ A♭ B♭ C D♭
C Augmented	C+	1, 3, 5♯	D .... D E F♯ G A B C♯ D
C Major Sixth	C6	1, 3, 5, 6	E♭ .... E♭ F G A♭ B♭ C D E♭
C Minor Sixth	Cm6	1, 3♭, 5, 6	E .... E F♯ G♯ A B C♯ D♯ E
C Dominant Seventh	C7	1, 3, 5, 7♭	F .... F G A B♭ C D E F
C Diminished Seventh	Cdim	1, 3♭, 5♭, 7♭♭	G♭ .... G♭ A♭ B♭ C♭ D♭ E♭ F G♭
C Major Seventh	Cmaj7	1, 3, 5, 7	G .... G A B C D E F♯ G
C Minor Seventh	Cm7	1, 3♭, 5, 7♭	A♭ .... A♭ B♭ C D♭ E♭ F G A♭
C Minor Seventh (With diminished fifth)	Cm7-5	1, 3♭, 5♭, 7♭	A .... A B C♯ D E F♯ G♯ A
C Augmented Seventh	C+7	1, 3, 5♯, 7♭	B♭ .... B♭ C D E♭ F G A B♭
C Ninth	C9	1, 3, 5, 7♭, 9	B .... B C♯ D♯ E F♯ G♯ A♯ B

Schaum Chord Dictionary

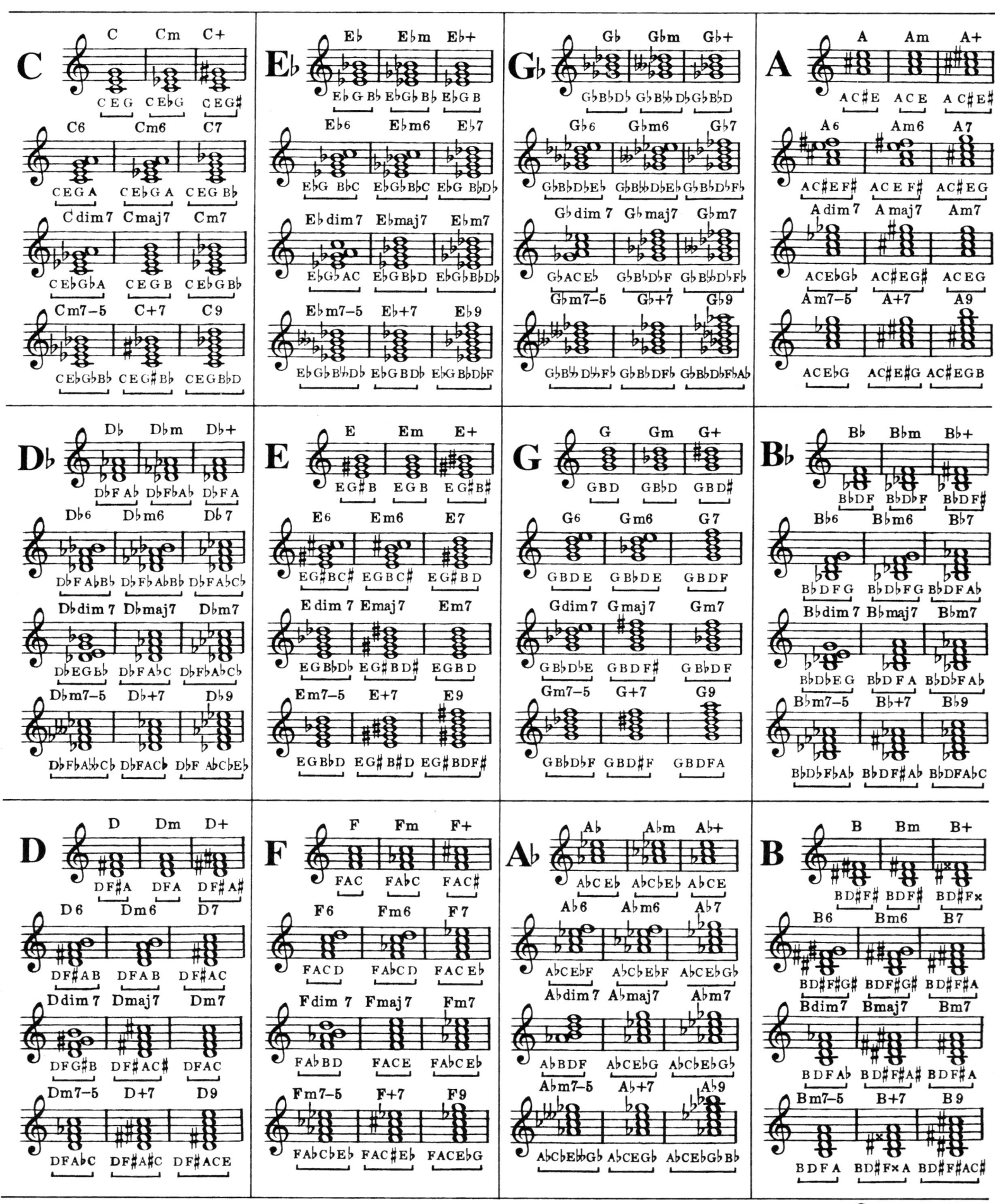

For F♯ chords use G♭   For G♯ chords use A♭   The letter names of the chords may be rearranged (inverted) if necessary.
For C♯ chords use D♭   For D♯ chords use E♭

For ease of note-reading, some of the chords above (especially diminished 7ths) have been notated enharmonically.